Penumbra

The Hollis Summers Poetry Prize

GENERAL EDITOR: DAVID SANDERS

Named after the distinguished poet who taught for many years at Ohio University and made Athens, Ohio, the subject of many of his poems, this competition invites writers to submit unpublished collections of original poems. The competition is open to poets who have not published a book-length collection as well as to those who have.

Full and updated information is available on the Hollis Summers Poetry Prize web page: ohioswallow.com/poetry_prize

Meredith Carson, *Infinite Morning*
Memye Curtis Tucker, *The Watchers*
V. Penelope Pelizzon, *Nostos*
Kwame Dawes, *Midland*
Allison Eir Jenks, *The Palace of Bones*
Robert B. Shaw, *Solving for X*
Dan Lechay, *The Quarry*
Joshua Mehigan, *The Optimist*
Jennifer Rose, *Hometown for an Hour*
Ann Hudson, *The Armillary Sphere*
Roger Sedarat, *Dear Regime: Letters to the Islamic Republic*
Jason Gray, *Photographing Eden*
Will Wells, *Unsettled Accounts*
Stephen Kampa, *Cracks in the Invisible*
Nick Norwood, *Gravel and Hawk*
Charles Hood, *South × South: Poems from Antarctica*
Alison Powell, *On the Desire to Levitate*
Shane Seely, *The Surface of the Lit World*
Michelle Y. Burke, *Animal Purpose*
Michael Shewmaker, *Penumbra*

Penumbra

Poems

Michael Shewmaker

OHIO UNIVERSITY PRESS

ATHENS

For Sarah —
In friendship and thanks.
So glad to meet you
and looking forward to
more of
your work.

Yours,

Shew

7/2017

Ohio University Press, Athens, Ohio 45701

ohioswallow.com
© 2017 by Michael Shewmaker

To obtain permission to quote, reprint, or otherwise reproduce or distribute
material from Ohio University Press publications, please contact our rights
and permissions department at (740) 593-1154 or (740) 593-4536 (fax).

Printed in the United States of America
Ohio University Press books are printed on acid-free paper ⊗ ™

27 26 25 24 23 22 21 20 19 18 17   5 4 3 2 1

Library of Congress Cataloging-in-Publication Data
Names: Shewmaker, Michael, author.
Title: Penumbra : poems / Michael Shewmaker.
Description: Athens, Ohio : Ohio University Press, [2017] | Series: The
  Hollis Summers poetry prize
Identifiers: LCCN 2016051640| ISBN 9780821422724 (hardback : acid-free
paper)
  | ISBN 9780821422731 (pbk : acid-free paper) | ISBN 9780821446041 (pdf)
Subjects: | BISAC: POETRY / American / General.
Classification: LCC PS3619.H486 A6 2017 | DDC 811/.6—dc23
LC record available at https://lccn.loc.gov/2016051640

Acknowledgments

Grateful acknowledgment is made to the editors of the journals in which these poems first appeared, sometimes in slightly different form: *Yale Review* ("The Lepidopterist," "Ink," "End of the Sermon"), *Virginia Quarterly Review* ("Horoscope for My Dying Father"), *Unsplendid* ("The Orchard," "The Devil in Grand Saline"), *storySouth* ("Harvest"), *Southwest Review* ("Winter Ghazal," "The Baptist"), *Sewanee Review* ("The Lover," "Diorama," "Advent"), *Sewanee Theological Review* ("The Choice"), *Parnassus* ("Babel"), *The Paris-American* ("Doppelgänger"), *Oxford American* ("The Pastor"), *The New Criterion* ("The Illusionist"), *Narrative* ("Photo Found on a Dead Man's Phone," "Intersection"), *Measure* ("The Artifact," "Crop Circles"), *Hopkins Review* ("Auguress"), *Hayden's Ferry Review* ("Overheard"), *The Freeman* ("La Llorona"), *The Dark Horse* ("On a Chinese Festival Scene Carved into the Casque of a Helmeted Hornbill"), *Crab Orchard Review* ("The Pastor's Wife"), *Columbia* ("The Somnambulist," "The Mime of Thermopylae"), *Birmingham Poetry Review* ("Tenebrae," "A Summer Primer," "The Neighbors Upstairs"), and *American Arts Quarterly* ("The Curlew").

"The Baptist" was selected as the winner of the 2013 Morton Marr Poetry Prize. "Auguress" was also published online at *Poetry Daily*. "Harvest," "Crop Circles," and "The Choice" also appeared in limited edition broadsides by Yellow Flag Press. "The Seven Thunders," "The Curlew," and "The Choice" appeared in *The Southern Poetry Anthology, Volume IV* (Texas Review Press, 2011).

Thanks also to Stanford University, Texas Tech University, and McNeese State University for generous fellowships and grants that allowed me to complete this book.

"The Choice" is for Aaron Kelly and Mike Wiley; "The Seven Thunders" is for Morri Creech; "The Orchard" is in memory of Virginia Shewmaker.

For the fallen

If in lyȝt we witnesse puyr devynyte,
þen shadowe herberwen our humanyte.

—Anonymous fragment, 14th century

Ses ailes de géant l'empêchent de marcher.

—Baudelaire, "The Albatross"

Contents

Doppelgänger

Who is this double goer, this familiar stranger
    following me with pockets full of moths—
        this moonlit strider, hawker who won't pass by
even when I pause to make a call—this changer
    of pace and posture, alley pisser with swaths
        of unrequited time?
                        What does he spy
in the limp rose on my lapel—in my unrest—
    the half-smoked cigarette, my borrowed clothes?

    Why must he check his pocket watch?
                                And why
must he escort me to my door in his pressed
        black tie?

One

Winter Ghazal

The longest month of the year is December.
Do you remember the nights of December?

I'm told in the town where we slept together,
the migrating geese still cry in December.

Bundled but cold in the freezing drizzle,
we tried to admire the lights of December.

Please tell me the story of the Pleiades—
those grieving sisters in the sky of December.

In the back of your closet, a single hanger.
The boom of the owl rewrites my December.

Rereading another unanswered letter,
you refuse to write a reply in December.

You always predicted the winds of winter.
The open window invites in December.

Michael, I'm asked, *in which month were you born?*
I was born in June—but I'll die in December.

Diorama

Stairs

Beneath the banister,
along the wall, two racks of shoes

and a tall, black grandfather clock.
Its face reads eight o'clock.

It chimes. A wooden woman
walks a small mechanical plank.

A row of portraits scales the stairs,
each larger than the last.

Bedroom

Greens and yellows. A man leans
hard on the bathroom door.

Covered in a ringed quilt,
the bed is meticulously made.

Too many pillows. Matching lamps
light the matching nightstands.

His hand jostles the knob.
Everything is in its place.

Kitchen

In the center of the room,
a table left in ruin—

a meal heaped on three plates,
a fourth shattered on the floor.

Milk trickles from a tiny mug
onto the tile. A dog

with different-colored eyes
licks cautiously along the grout.

Hallway

Down the narrow corridor,
more portraits, a glass case

lined with porcelain dolls,
a runner leading toward a door

latched against the dark. A lone
light glows beneath the dolls.

They float above their stands,
ordered in descending rows.

Bathroom

The vanity reflects
the floral trimming. Violets.

A woman, sitting with her back
to the door, hides her eyes.

Behind the half-drawn curtain
in a clawfoot tub, the children wait—

propped on its lip like cherubs—here,
where no one will cry out.

The Neighbors Upstairs

They only stirred at night while we were sleeping.
In a small space that must have mirrored ours,
they moved freely between the muted hours—
my father's snoring and my mother's weeping.
Like the tired gods that pace above this city—
abolished and forgotten by the hand
that shaped them, prodigals who understand
the gravity of loss—they showed no pity
for those who slept beneath them.
                                    From the vent,
a tremolo of words—though indistinct,
distorted by the duct, yet somehow linked
to longing—kept me up with their intent.

But now that I am older, torn by choices,
it's difficult to sleep without their voices.

The Lover

presses his ear against the thinnest wall
of his apartment. In the empty space
between, he hears a static like the sea's.

Past that—above the television's talk
she always falls asleep to—a loud clock
tallies the gradual hours.
                                    He waits until
she rouses for a drink, washes her face,
removes her lenses. Then he pulls away,
paces the hall again.
                                The Cabernet
he bartered from a girl with scarlet lips
just west of the canal—outside of Lille—
lies uncorked on the counter. Overhead,
the fan wheels freely in the dark.
                                            The dead,
he thinks, must make for patient lovers. He
should go to bed.
                        This late, the distant ships—
the quiet chore of their unmooring—sound
to him like her when no one is around,

when, loosening her robe by slow degrees—
as he unloops and coils his belt now—she
presses her ear firmly against the wall.

Ink

Is there a canvas crueler than the body?
The ink is permanent. The skin is not.
I have no patience for the lover's gaudy
heart—swollen, pierced—a hackneyed blot
beating against the odds. I've seen them all:
straddled by seraphim, or torn apart—
on women, men, the lesser parlor's wall—
hallmarked MOM, or skewered by a dart
from Cupid's quiver.
                    But enough of love.
I work in monochrome. I deal in skulls.
Behind each piece a brief, familiar story.
It ends in bones—the sort of plot that dulls
the point. My needle's steadiest above
a stinging script that reads:
                    Memento Mori.

The Illusionist

Without the usual work of wands,
she dazzles solely with her hands.

The coin behind your ear is gone.
Her turtledoves have turned to stone.

She plucks the rose from her corsage,
your ring tucked in its petaled cage.

She knows your card. She levitates.
The coin appears in duplicates.

And though she makes a show of it—
the scripted struggle, the long wait—

no locks or chains are sound enough
to bind her to this stage. And though

you know the limits of the eye,
her sleight of hand, the hidden lie,

you choose to see as through a sieve.
You still applaud. You still believe.

The Artifact

They dredged it from the bottom of the sea,
   a copper cube—a barnacled machine,
   cogs stopped, teeth patinaed by the brine.
The lifework of an unknown Ptolemy,
it baffled all who saw it. *An odd clock,*
   they thought, *an orrery.* They ordered tests,
   redrew schemata, scoured the oldest texts
for origin—but they could not unlock
   its mechanism.
             Only in the mind
of one who stands before its artifice—
   awestruck by the broken clockwork, blind
to time's strict theorem etched into its face—
   and eyes shut—determined to unlearn
   the dogma of that law—the great gears turn.

Intersection

A boat-tailed grackle counts the passing cars
from the traffic light it perches on.
The ferryman of Fairmont Avenue,
its eyes are scars.
                    Dark's impoverished son,
it covets coins—the tolls that it is due—
glinting on dashes, lodged in seats. Its head
is cocked. The light is yellow. Its wings, spread.

Two

The Curlew

Plate 357 (Numenius borealis) *is the only instance in which
the subject appears dead in the work of John James Audubon.*

1.

Beneath the cedars stirring in the churchyard,
stone angels endure the weather for the dead
while townsmen, slinging shovelfuls of dirt,
stoop in a selfsame rhythm. He waits alone,
sketching the angels from the shade — *a kind
of heavenly bird,* he reasons with himself —
although their wings are broken, faces scarred,
each fragile mouth feigning the same sad smile
as the one before it. Offered triple his price
to paint a likeness of the pastor's daughter —
buried for more than a week — he reluctantly
agreed — times being what they are. The men
call from the grave — beckon with their hands
calloused and swollen with the wage of work.

2.

The nervous bird worries the waterline,
probing the sand between the waves' retreat
and surge. Its shrill call dies into a wind
that scours the wide, airy stretch of shore.
How dull it seems against the gulf — with no
raised crest or striking plumage to admire,
no flamboyant breast or ivory bill,
only the markings of a common shorebird.
And yet he studies it — from behind the dunes —
studies its several postures, grounded and
in sudden flight — and not content to praise

it from a distance, to sacrifice detail,
unpacks his brushes and arranges them
before raising his rifle and taking aim.

3.
The men still beckon from the grave. The angels
seem expectant. In the walk between the shade
and where they wait, he thinks, for the first time,
of the work ahead. The men, who moments ago
joked about worms and the girl's virginity,
delicately scrape the remaining dirt and clay
off the coffin's lid. They sweep the lacquer
with their hands. The cedars rattle overhead.
And while they struggle with the lid, he vows
to recreate her—as she might have been—
to ignore her blemishes—whatever they
may be: the jutting cheekbones of her face,
her sunken skin—to find the form that once
was there, and, afterward, erase what was.

4.
Wings stiffening against its breast, the curlew
refuses the rigging. Driven by the sun's descent,
a lack of wood, and never being one to work
from memory, he lays it in the sand
beyond the tide's tall reach. Nothing escapes
his hand: from alien feet to modest crown,
the upturned wing and speckled down, the throat,
the slender curve of beak—the small, dark eye.
He thinks it wears its body like a cloak—
or like the white gown draped loosely around
the pastor's daughter, the shadow of the cedars
branching over her folded hands, her chest,
her exposed neck and clavicles—her face
still radiant as if she might sit up to greet him.

On a Chinese Festival Scene Carved into the Casque of a Helmeted Hornbill

Between the valleys where its eyes had been,
as if etched into a sheet of polished jade
or lapis lazuli, on the wide bridge
that spans the river which divides the village,
the farmers listen as the planters' songs
ripen in the round mouths of the musicians.

They sing the story of the harvest, the story
of their ancestors—who stooped above
the same tepid paddies, beneath the same
slate sky before the hornbills' late migrations—
who also gathered at this river, around
the drying rice, to sing this time of year.

While the elders croon along, their eyes
tired and glittering, and while the men
tend to the mealtime fires, and the women,
still robed in their wet dresses, swing like sickles
to the music—the children, glad to be alone,
race their paper boats beneath the bridge.

Beyond the village, beyond the last held note
of the final song, above the pale horizon
like a still sun, dear reader, you are like
the artist, leaning above the dead bird's skull,
who must have thought, if only once,
The greatest art is carved in bone.

Harvest

Ruth speaks in old age

To watch him in the fields,
his tempered violence
against the grain, the long
silent sweep of the scythe,
the gathering of sheaves,
recalls a happiness
brief as kindled chaff.

Beneath the tilting sun,
the same strict sun of childhood,
bound by the rhythm of
his labor, he ignores
the frailness of his body,
the failing light, his shadow
rising slowly to meet him.

How long will the moon stall
over the edge of the fields?
The day-moon, a lone ghost
above the grain? The stalks
stir in a subtle wind
that starts along the length
of the descending blade —

and as the barley yields
to the wide arc of his
endeavoring, it whispers
in another tongue,
and of another time,
when, like the grain, he laid
me on the threshing floor.

Crop Circles

How strange to find them in the failing dark,
    to scan the rows for a trace of answer.
The scarecrow points both ways. It hides a smirk.
How strange to find them. In the failing dark,
crows wheel above its prop, awkwardly shirk
    its stare. They multiply like cancer.
How strange. To find them in the failing dark,
    scan the rows for a trace of answer.

Automaton

I am the voice of gears that turn against
    the hollow ticking of the clock. I am
a copper song, the tinny comb's teeth
    plucked in a rosewood box.
                    I am the hum
    and curiosity of cams, the thrum
of countless cylinders at work beneath
a form shaped by and for yourself,
                       condensed
    into a small boy's body. Wound, I am
as you would have me: flawed, by fits and starts,
an argument against a golden mean.
                    A *doll,*
    you said, *designed to imitate a thought—*
a thought I may have had
                had I been taught
to question my creator's hand. To fall
    a man must first attempt to stand. I am
my father's son—the sum of all my parts.

A Summer Primer

Before the Internet, we borrowed books
from libraries. You joked that we'd go blind.
We met beneath the bridge for furtive looks
at bodies not our own. We longed to find
the logic in those glossy pages. *Lock
and key*, you said. You mocked the illustrations
but watched me while I read. The mossy rock
still marks our cache, our buried educations.
Have you forgotten this?
                Nevertheless,
returning home, I often think of when—
that afternoon—I asked you to undress
and the cold creek mirrored your silver skin,
the shivering shapes of our uncertainties,
your tangled hair the color of spring bees.

Nocturne

The owl recounts the phases of the moon.
Tonight its song is gibbous, almost full,
and for the weary child, who cannot sleep,
it starts too soon.
            Who knows night's old rule
more than this boy?—this bird that will not keep
its quiet? Both bound by their own concerns,
the owl calls—the child tosses, turns.

Three

The Baptist

May I sit down? My knees are killing me
and—if I'm not mistaken—you seem like
you wouldn't mind a stranger's company.
Besides, I'll soon be boarding for El Paso,
where conversation's an abandoned well,
and I'd be glad to chat myself. You been?
It's hardly worth the trip if you ask me.
I make it every year and every year
it's hotter than the year before. But hell,
here it's as hot as sin.
                         Which seems as good
a place to start as any . . . *Sin*, I mean.
Don't worry, son. I'm no evangelist.
Just try to think of this as *my* confession.

You strike me as the praying type—soft eyes
and no tattoos—but one who's lost his way.
I understand. I've loitered in my share
of pews and hid my issues with the Lord.
Granted, mine may turn the stomach more
than most, but like the good book says, a sin
is sin.
        You seem uncomfortable. Despite
what's said about me on the ten o'clock,
I make my choices carefully. You're not
my type. At least, you're not today. Relax.
It always happens differently—but some
particulars don't change.
                          You ever had
a vision? Not the sort the psychic squawks

27

about behind her ball, but something more
internal, learned even, like déjà vu—
but not exactly. It's more biblical
than that—as if, behind your eyes, the seed
of sleeping scripture bursts into bold bloom.
(That's *if*, of course, you're a believing man.)
The sun might sink behind that single cloud
and—though we're hardly in the heat of August—
those three oaks across the road might shed
their brittle leaves, almost at once, which—fixed
however briefly in their fall—explode
into a flock of crows that scatter through
and from the naked branches. Soon they're all
I see. The birds. Then nothing—only darkness.
And then I watch the final scene played out
in some dark theater of the mind—projected
against the backdrop of a raven's wing.

This all while sitting next to you, while talking
freely as we have been. Relax. There's nothing
doing. No crows or falling leaves. Besides,
there's no water for miles—although a sink
or toilet gets the job done in a pinch.
I'm only kidding—and, truth is, these things
take time. I wait. I make their lives my own.
Take Maryanne, for instance—mother of two,
divorced. She was a shy one. Her tears told
the story of her childhood: how, refusing
to say Amen at night, she hoped communion
would last, at least, till morning.
                                    And the more
I know about their lives, the more I feel
the world's weight shifting beneath the water.
And after—after the tremors, the last gasp

for air, the body slowly letting go—
a peace that passes all our understanding.

But words are useless in these instances.
Words, words . . . *My word*, my father used to say
when tried a little. He was a Baptist preacher.
Does that surprise you? He's how I had my start.
I watched him every Sunday—still attend
as often as I can—until his heart
refused to let him work the baptistry.
He asked if I would help. It was, I thought,
an obedient son's responsibility.
Of course, it made for a few awkward Sundays.
When he asked why I held them down so long,
I said I wanted to make sure the change
was permanent—which, I suppose, was not
a lie.
          But that's when I began to take
Christ's Rule seriously . . . *Do unto others*
as you would have them do to you. You see,
I dream of drowning nearly every night—
it truly is a beautiful way to die—
but that's too simple, selfish, immature.

I'm sure you're wondering why. Why tell you this?
Truth is, I thought I saw a younger version
of myself, something kindred, in your eyes—
maybe the love of a forbidden art?
Truth is, I've looked for you for quite some time.
I'm getting old and tired. I can't keep on.
My water's drawn inside the house of God.

Come, come . . . and I will gladly be your first—
that you might rise and walk in this new life.

The Devil in Grand Saline

One never tires of the old tonks in Texas.
Tonight, while hunting for a souvenir,
I chased my second whiskey with a beer
and overheard a man whose girlfriend's Lexus—
the one *he* bought—keeps turning up around
his son's apartment. "Cooper, you can quote
me here. I'll slit that little bastard's throat."
I laughed and ordered them another round.

"Something funny, stranger?"
                                                    "Well," I said,
"I've heard that line before. It's seldom true."
"That so?"
                    "It is."
                                    He shot his Scotch and threw
the tumbler. "C'mon, Coop. This place is dead."
They skipped their tab and stumbled to his truck.

My dear, drunk Abraham—I wish you luck.

Babel

Weightless, the winter constellations tower
      above our poor-lit city. Smoothing the drapes
         she chose for him, I cannot find the words.
Night is a lesson we must learn, I wrote
      in verse. (She stills his cradle, folds the spread.)
         And worse, *The moonlight is a subtle sword.*

There is no answer in this room—where, silent,
      we readied for our unborn son. And now,
         to endure the hours our loss has won,
she stacks his blocks to spell his name. *Listen:*
         Our grief is what we own.

An Apostate's Prayer

I wake to your shape in every shadow, Father.
  My wavering conscience stalks me like a ghost,
an unnamed saint who died
                too soon, an only son.

But when, at mass, I take the offering of your Son—
  the wine, the wafer—that your will be done—Father,
I doubt it all: the sacring bell,
              the crumbling host,

the body tasteless on the tongue, the lineage lost
  between the briar and a vine. Even your Son,
remember, cried out on his cross.
             Forsake *me*, Father,

in the name of the Father, Son, and Holy Ghost.

The Pastor's Wife

*By night on my bed I sought him who my soul
loveth: I sought him but I found him not.*

—Song of Solomon 3:1

Lord—since he has forgotten how to love
your faithful servant, whom you gave to share
the burden of his work, to sweat, to prove
the glory of your word, and since I'm sure
by now he has forgotten the sweet tongues
of our private Pentecost, the narrow bed
abandoned in our rapture, the arched rungs
of my back, "Jacob's ladder," the sacred bread
we broke and ate together, since our marriage
rots like the carcass without honey, since
you say I shouldn't blame him for this bondage,
despite my will to please, my constant hints,
and since I couldn't lie to you—it's true:
because I can't blame him, Lord, I blame you.

The Lepidopterist

The year before the long divorce, she framed
his dearest species—the White Witch, the Atlas,
the Clouded-bordered Brindle—matted each
in black, and hung
               them carefully among
the portraits on their bedroom wall. To teach
herself to love, she read about his practice—
examined diagrams, minutiae named.
                          But,
when she lay close, he sweat beneath the spread,
and, stirring to her heat, he dreamt in grays—
of garish wings unfolding to disclose
the owlish eyes
              of the Io: those bright lies
burning above their bed. Against the windows,
the wild moths bred. She never slept—her gaze
unchanged. *Are you awake?* she often said.

The Somnambulist

Always a startle in the dark. I wake
            to visions worse than dreams:
a brick in hand and bleeding feet, an ache

        for answers and the screams
of sirens nearing from a distant street—
            or, once, to the extremes

of autumn air and an oppressive heat,
            the stench of gasoline,
wind ripening a field of burning wheat.

        Weary of that routine,
of stirring to an aftermath of me,
            I learned to trust caffeine,

amphetamines, and cigarettes to see
            me through another night.
But, as you know, sleep wins eventually.

        Weak and head-heavy, sight
goes first—before the mind can comprehend
            the failure of the light.

Deprived, my briefest dreams turn violent.
            Forgive me. When I woke
tonight—or *if* I woke—my fingers bent

around your throat, the cloak
of evening in your eyes, I couldn't take
    the chance—or wouldn't—smoke

billowing from beneath your bedroom door.
    They'll be here soon. I'm sure
you understand. Some dreams you can't ignore.

La Llorona

She hears a voice across the water.
And weeping to remember, gowned
in gray, she can't recall her daughter.

Her candle wavers on the altar.
They say that she was never found.
She hears a voice. Across the water,

the trees harbor a darker weather.
An oarless rowboat runs aground
and drifts again. And like her daughter,

she wades into the drowsy river—
stone-pocketed, without a sound.
She hears a voice beneath the water

that lingers like a lover's. Laughter
almost—but softer, colder, drowned
by the shy whimpering of a daughter

who understands that what comes after
is like the weeping of a wound.
She hears the voice. Her only daughter.
They'll drag her body from the water.

Tenebrae

Sedlec Ossuary

The chandelier of bones affords a light
as scrupulous as de la Tour's. Beneath
the ossein garlands, the files of grinning teeth,
one loses sight
          of what this place is for.
Why mind the monstrance at the altar? Or fall
onto our knees to pray? And still we call
this bone-house holy. We pay to pace this floor.

Four

Overheard

"When he went missing on the eve before
the fourth," Miss Vera said, "it wasn't news.
He liked to cat around, although no more
than other boys who filled the rearmost pews.
Still, there was a queer air about it all—
and he was known to filch a pound of bacon,
or two, occasionally from the butcher's stall,
or welch on petty bets that he had taken
but couldn't quite recall.
                                    Poor Percy," she said.
"Poor Percival . . .
                            But what else could we do
the night we fished him from our silo, dead,
drowned in our father's corn? What *could* we do?"
(She loved to tell it, but shivered while she told it.)
"We buried him. We sacked the grain and sold it."

Digging My Father's Grave

The rich clay reeks. The spade
        weighs more than I remember.
                I know of no one who
                        has bent like this to break
ground in an alder's shade,
        to measure love's last labor
                by shovelfuls—the few
                        late hours the task will take.

Surely it happens still—
        and must be happening now—
                somewhere where sons are meant
                        to reckon the dead men
who made them, sons who stall
        above a stone, who know
                exhaustion in the scent
                        of soil, the wage of sin.

A son becomes his father
        through certain scrims of light,
                as when he draws a curtain
                        before the sun expires
and airy as a feather,
        the trailing fabric—bright
                and sheer-spun with a satin
                        damask—refines its fires.

How deep is deep enough?
        How wide? And why not lay
                the shovel down instead?

The alder understands
what I cannot. And though
      I tire of this clay,
            my father is not dead—
                  and these are not his hands.

The Orchard

Where has all the windfall gone?
she asks in my recurring dream.
I lead her by the arm. Her gown,
lined in a bronze light, glides above

the lawn. Her feet are wet with dew.
I want to answer with the truth,
but know that she is hungry—and
afraid. Instead, I clench my teeth.

She's forgotten the fruit's name,
and thinks that I'm my father—last
of her two sons and daughter. Time
is relative among these trees

that stretch as far as we can see,
smoldering like Eden in the sun.
Before I wake, she asks again,
Where has all the windfall gone?

Auguress

The pendulum of her clock keeps perfect time.
Impatient, propped against the windowsill,
she waits for noon, for flights departing north
from the neighboring airport. As they climb,
their steel bellies drag broad shadows across
her lawn. She fidgets as the garden dims:
her roses and the untrimmed clematis,
the hanging feeder—her entire street
darkens beneath the turbines' hiss.
                                    Before
and after, she often wonders where they go—
imagines conversations, attendants neat
and eager, rows of smiles as sharp as scythes—
but while their passing shadows briefly fill
her empty teacup to its brim—she knows.

The Choice

In August, when the drapes seem sheer
against the light of noon and shadows
shrink beneath the wilting leaves
of ivy, the gathering birds repeat
their lists of ritual agitations.
Such is their sole inheritance:
a bred desire and fear of silence.

Who can blame the mockingbird
for borrowing the cardinal's song?
I've heard it in the afternoons,
and, unaware, when wandering
alone from room to vacant room,
paused by the phone or in a doorway
and delighted in its music;

and surely she has heard it too,
my neighbor—the widowed curator—
who, haunted by an artist's hunger,
spends her pittance on supplies,
her evenings crouched beneath
a naked bulb to paint again
the likeness of Renoir's *La Loge*.

The heat presses against the panes.
The birds retreat into the leaves.
Perhaps there is no new beauty
in this landscape—only shades
of the forgotten—yet we search
for it, beneath the unexpected
flash of the mockingbird's ascent.

Horoscope for My Dying Father

Shortly, you'll wake into the room
you woke to over half your life.

The light will inch across the ceiling
until it meets the wall.
                              The sheets
will seem softer than you remember.

Your lover will be dreaming still
and you will rise without a sound.

Back to the mirror, you will dress
in your finest black attire.
                              Outside,
though we can't see it in this light,
the colossal wheel will still turn.

When, finally, you descend the stairs,
the warped risers will not creak.

You'll pause before the door, unlock
it—check the clock.
                              Until then, sleep.

School Bus Graveyard

Their carcasses decay beneath the weather.
Honeysuckle crowds the wheel wells, snakes
around their sagging axles. The sun strips
their paint and splits the leather.
                              What wrecks
are these that once were counted on? Dead ships
on a dry sea? At evening, when I pass,
I see small hands and faces in the glass.

Five

The Seven Thunders

> *And when the seven thunders spoke, I was about to write;*
> *but I heard a voice from heaven say, "Seal up what the seven*
> *thunders have said and do not write it down."*
>
> —Revelation 10:4

1.

There is no rain. Not yet.
Only these clouds that drift
above my father's pasture —
swelling with the low voice
of anticipated thunder.

2.

The hidden past uncoils
like the bright copperhead
that scarred my father's hand.
It slept beneath the spigot —
tail twitching as it dreamt.

3.

I feared that seething hand —
the seven seals that coursed
in his blood, the raised vein
pulsing as he cursed
the clouds, the lack of rain.

4.

Father, why must you reckon
the silence between thunders?
Why whisper to the air
the measured Mississippis
you echo like a prayer?

5.
And when I asked, afraid,
what the thunders were,
he pressed my palms together
as one who understands—
"Our Lord, clapping his hands."

6.
Above the burning dropseed,
a copperhead hangs dead
on the top strand of barbed-wire—
and straddling it, the shrike
that sings my father's name.

7.
The final peal fades
over the blistered pasture,
over the shadeless grave
where grass has never grown,
and rain pelts the dry stone.

Advent

His mother must have looked away,
the reckless boy who teeters on
the railing of the balcony.

Beneath him, the congregation sings
a final hymn in a minor key.

Above, the oculus, gold leaf,
the folded wings of Gabriel.

Impossible to say what lured
him from his seat—the choir's appeal
or the angel's feet?
                    What is his name
so we might call him, safely, down—
this child who balances between

what cannot and what can be seen,
the martyrs and the marbled ground?

Destin Wedding

No shade. The groomsmen squint in the harsh light
reflecting off the sand. The bridesmaids, sunburnt,
sweat beading on their chests, adjust their dresses
and fan themselves. The planner checks her watch,
signals the bride. And during her brief march—
rehearsed until perfected, until sincere—
the groom fingers his boutonniere.
                                                    It is
the surf, however, that demands the guests'
attention. The break and swell of the rising tide—
only a few feet from the makeshift altar—
drown Mozart's *Minuet in G*. The bride
laughs; the groom smiles. But when the pastor
asks if any might have reason—the waves
insist on their uninterrupted say.

The Pastor

*The sun will be turned to darkness and
the moon to blood before the coming
of the great and dreadful day of the Lord.*

—Joel 2:31

I've seen enough of your creation, Lord,
its absurd conceits, the sins of idle men
ripened to gnashing teeth. The winter wren
has built its nest elsewhere. And we've ignored
the image we were made in, the divine breath
that stirred the clay. Why must you tarry, Lord?
Sound your trumpet. Raise your flaming sword.
Remind us what it means to fear a death
and a return. Your bride has taken to whoring,
and, like the cheapest whore in Chickasaw,
she makes a killing—behind your deacons' doors.
It is time, Lord. The pale horse is snoring
in its stall. Strike a match and light the straw.
And not because it's my will, Lord, but yours.

Übermensch

In Naumburg, beneath the spires
that rise along the Saale, behind
the abandoned factory
where bright machines once stitched
the ragged hems of eyeless bears,
in front of a house with lofty gables
and sculpted gardens, Nietzsche juggles
two smoking chainsaws
and a bowling pin.

His mustache twitches as he chants—
Oh Mensch! Gieb Acht!
Was spricht die tiefe Mitternacht?
Not one to give to gravity,
he adds a pair of pruning shears
to complicate his theory.
The chainsaws chirp around his ears.
And on his chin,
he balances the bowling pin.

Quick! Someone throw the man a fish,
a steering wheel! Who cares?
He's hardly sweating. His orbit
is all too perfect—
Doch alle Lust will Ewigkeit
will tiefe, tiefe Ewigkeit!
Hurry! Before the blind sky falls
and all is only ashes, now,
before he risks his final bow.

The Mime of Thermopylae

"The prophet's job is simply to speak . . ."

She hears them in her sleep: the smoldering gates
    grating against the cavern floor.
        Impossible to tell
    which way the hinges swing—toward fire
or the retreating sea—she prays and waits.

Mornings she performs for bordering towns
    while heedless bakers stoke their stoves
        and women queue into
    the streets to buy the bitter loaves.
With her hands, she frames her gravest frowns.

The children take her for a harlequin.
    Her priest assures her that a fool
        with talents to distract
    may someday prove an oracle.
Until then, though, she plays the charlatan:

She clamps a withered rose between her teeth
    and musters all the art of gesture,
        as if the flames of Hell
    were stitched into the trailing vesture
of her long, borrowed cape—darker than death—

and whirling, whirling like a burning top—
    a wisp of smoke drawn toward a fan
        or up a baker's flue—
    briefly becomes the final FIN
before she wobbles and her tired arms drop.

The children clap but promptly turn to play—
    and the gates grate inside the caves.
        (Her act is not an act.)
    They open toward the meager waves.
Hear her—though she has nothing left to say.

The Cooling Pond

Chernobyl, 1988

Dead reeds crackle like a Geiger counter
along the shore. The glaring sun descends
behind the striped stack of Reactor 4.
But in this rusty water, few have seen
these fenced remains. As through an older lens—
before the fallout—red pines appear green
again. The pluming thunderhead seems more
than ashes, or the promise of a downpour,
an erasure.
        But this is not a testament
of new beginnings. Even the birds have gone.
And still, beneath this surface, through the murk,
below the coils and cooling core—alone—
starving in the contaminated dark,
a gilled shape stirs beneath the sediment.

Photo Found on a Dead Man's Phone

A field. No clouds. Tall grasses bend
toward the foreground. In the distance,
three pheasants break above the brush,
against the wind.
                     What brief persistence
could capture this—the sudden flush
of wings, the late light that defined them—
the shadow of the man, the sun behind him?

The End of the Sermon

I came to in the middle of the pasture.
Rain ticked against the tractor's hood and steam
coiled above the chassis. Thunder plowed
into the distance where the clouds obscured
the day's remaining light.
                                        It was a Sunday.
I'd preached on perseverance—on Paul's thorn—
and, afterward, had hoped to mow the thistle
before the storm. I don't recall much more
than that: only the distant scent of rain,
the way the thistle sloughed its seed beneath
the blade, the hackles rising on my neck
before the strike I also don't recall.

Before that afternoon, I'd often answer—
when asked about my calling, how I'd known—
Some men are drawn to heaven. Others heaven
won't leave alone.
                                And so, I stay indoors.
I count in Mississippis the slow seconds
between retreating thunders, skim the last
chapters of Revelation to forget
the trying absence of that pasture—time
I lost—until I finally nod off . . .

But even in my sleep I see the pasture.
In the persistent dream, I'm looking out
the attic dormer, where, beyond the fence-line,
a narrow stand of longleaf pines sways
under the gathering clouds—when, only just

before I turn away, a bright shank strikes
the tallest of the farthest trees.
                              It leans
and since I am removed, behind the glass,
since all is still, it falls in utter silence.

Who knows the awful mind of our creator?
I've seen that pine fall every night since then,
and every night I fail to hear the voice
inside that quiet.
                    But what is there to hear?
I'm through with prayer. Please don't misunderstand.
I only mean to say that had you woke
like me, nameless and shivering in the rain,
you might consider what you're asking for —
the steep price of briefly becoming light.

I came to in the middle of the pasture.
The tractor idled in the slackening rain.
I didn't dream — or else, I don't remember.
I spoke a single word. There was no answer.